TIMELINES

annuals

1990

by
Jane Duden

CRESTWOOD HOUSE

New York

Maxwell Macmillan Canada
Toronto

Maxwell Macmillan International
New York Oxford Singapore Sydney

Library of Congress Catalog Card Number

92-72890

Photo Credits
Cover: All photos courtesy of AP—Wide World Photos.

CRESTWOOD HOUSE

Macmillan Publishing Company
866 Third Avenue
New York, NY 10022

Maxwell Macmillan Canada, Inc.
1200 Eglinton Avenue East
Suite 200
Don Mills, Ontario M3C 3N1

Macmillan Publishing Company is part of the Maxwell Communication Group of Companies.

Produced by Flying Fish Studio

Printed in the United States of America

First edition

10 9 8 7 6 5 4 3 2 1

CONTENTS

On the cover: Celebrating Earth Day 1990

The beginning of the end—a protest in Russia

INTRODUCTION

From Earth Day to the crisis in the Persian Gulf, 1990 was a loaded year! As the 1990s got underway, millions around the world renewed the call to protect the planet. Even before Earth Day it seemed that the 1990s would be the Decade of the Environment. It looked like it would also bring a new era in world affairs. The Communist Soviet empire began to collapse. It struggled with a crumbling economy and a growing demand for independence from its republics. East and West Germany were reunited after a 45-year division. Movements toward freedom and democracy changed the face of Eastern and central Europe. Crisis in the Persian Gulf brought the United States and many other nations to the brink of war with Iraq as the year closed.

The 1990 census showed there were nearly 250 million Americans, with Hispanic Americans the fastest growing minority. But experts feared the count was off because many homeless people were missed in the counting.

There was good news and bad news in space exploration. In sports, records were made and broken. And new things were "in" for the kids of 1990. Find out about these stories and more in the pages ahead!

JANUARY

SPACE EXPLORATION

The U.S. space shuttle *Columbia* lifted off on January 9 with a crew of five. Their mission: to launch a new communications satellite. The astronauts also rescued a scientific satellite that had been in space for nearly six years with test materials. The crew returned to Earth on January 20. It was the longest shuttle mission to date—ten days, 21 hours.

The Simpsons

"DON'T HAVE A COW, MAN"

The Simpsons became a weekly Sunday-night hit television show in 1990. The outrageous statements of the family's young son, Bart, were heard on playgrounds across the country. The wild success of *The Simpsons* proved that animated features were no longer just kids' stuff.

SUPER BOWL XXIV

On January 28 the San Francisco 49ers won their second Super Bowl in two years. Led by quarterback Joe Montana, the 49ers beat the Denver Broncos, 55–10. Jerry Rice caught seven passes for 148 yards and a Super Bowl record—three touchdowns. Montana threw a record five touchdown passes. He won the Super Bowl's Most Valuable Player award for the third time.

Joe Montana tosses one off.

GOLDEN ARCHES IN RUSSIA

Moscow's first McDonald's opened on January 30. Soviet citizens lined up to buy Big Macs and french fries!

McDonald's opens in Moscow.

Bill Shoemaker

THE SHOE'S LAST RIDE

Jockey Bill Shoemaker rode his last race February 3 at Santa Anita Park in Arcadia, California. He retired after the race, ending a 41-year career. During those years, nine men had been in the White House, and the United States had fought in two wars and added two states. "The Shoe" won a record 8,833 races, and he had $123 million in earnings.

Nelson and Winnie Mandela

HERO BRINGS HOPE TO A TROUBLED LAND

On February 11 Nelson Mandela became a free man. The black leader had spent more than 27 years in a South African prison. Mandela had been jailed for leading blacks against South Africa's white-dominated government. His release was a sign of hope for racial equality in the troubled country. During the year, he visited the U.S. and many other countries to speak about better lives for all racial groups.

During 1990, efforts to end apartheid—strict racial segregation—continued. By October the government of South Africa had opened public hospitals, parks, beaches and other areas to all races.

BUCKLE UP, BUT DON'T LIGHT UP

On February 25 smoking was banned on domestic U.S. airline flights of less than six hours. The ban was partly due to a 1986 report from the U.S. Surgeon General. The report stressed the dangers of smoking for smokers and for nonsmokers who breathe second-hand smoke in a closed area.

1990
MARCH

SIX ACROSS ANTARCTICA

Explorers on skis and dogsleds completed the International Trans-Antarctica Expedition on March 3. Six men from six nations did what others had tried and failed to do. They made the first crossing of Antarctica by dogsled. The seven-month journey began in July 1989. The men and their 40 dogs went through the worst weather in the world. They were battered by storms with winds reaching 90 miles an hour. They were frostbitten by temperatures as low as -45° Fahrenheit. They were worn out by 3,700 miles of brutal terrain.

Why did they do it? Adventure was one reason. More important, they wanted to focus people's attention on Antarctica—the world's last pure wilderness. Antarctica is governed by the Antarctic Treaty. Signed by 26 nations, it says that Antarctica may be used only for peaceful and scientific reasons. The treaty, originally written in 1959, was coming up for review. Nations were debating whether they should explore for oil and other minerals on Antarctica or whether the whole continent should become a wilderness park. The explorers wanted to convince people that protecting the environment is the right choice. Their efforts were successful; on October 4, 1991, member nations agreed to ban mining and oil exploration on Antarctica for at least the next 50 years.

LONG LOST DISCOVERY

In March a scientist photographed a hairy-eared dwarf lemur on the island of Madagascar. The tiny primate, only 7 1/2 inches (14 centimeters) long, had never before been seen alive. Scientists feared it was extinct.

Today, many tropical rain forest plants and animals are becoming extinct. Entire species vanish as their rain-forest habitats are destroyed for homes, farms, mining and timber. Discovery of the tiny lemur was good news. It meant a chance to protect a rare animal from becoming extinct.

SHE'S A SMASH!

At the Virginia Slims tennis tournament in Florida in March 1990, 13-year-old Jennifer Capriati became the youngest player ever to reach the finals of a professional women's tennis tournament. Capriati also reached the semifinals of the 1990 French Open, one of the most important tournaments in tennis, and she became the youngest player to win a main-draw match at Wimbledon.

Jennifer Capriati

VALDEZ CAPTAIN PUNISHED

A jury in Alaska found Joseph J. Hazelwood guilty in connection with the largest oil spill in U.S. history. Hazelwood was the captain of the oil tanker *Exxon Valdez*, which spilled about 11 million gallons of oil into Prince William Sound in March 1989. The oil spill hurt the area's fishing industry. It killed thousands of sea creatures. Though Hazelwood was cleared of the most serious charges, he was ordered to pay Alaska $50,000 and spend 1,000 hours cleaning oily beaches.

Joseph Hazelwood

1990
APRIL

COUNTING AMERICANS

All the people in the United States were counted on April 1, 1990. Once every ten years, the U.S. government carries out a population census. A census is an official count of the people in a country. A census form is sent to every household in the United States. The forms have questions that everyone is supposed to answer. When added up, the figures from everyone's answers tell us a lot about our country, like which states and cities gained or lost people. Census counts are often the basis for allocating funds and services. The numbers are also used to tell how many seats each state should have in the House of Representatives.

When machines added up the numbers, the population of the United States was nearly 250 million. But some people thought that the final count was too low. Many people did not return the forms, and experts said that many homeless people were not counted. They also said that thousands of blacks, Hispanics and other people in large cities, such as New York and Chicago, were left out.

The government wanted to adjust the incorrect census. In some areas a recount was done, and experts planned to adjust the count in some cities. New counts were to be based on information known about the people living there. This kind of adjustment had never before been done. Experts are working on ways to make the next census, in 2000, more accurate.

SORRY CHARLIE, TRUTH IN LABELING

Nets used for tuna fishing can drown dolphins by the thousands, and people who care about dolphins are angry about it. In April U.S. tuna canners responded to demands for tuna caught without harm to dolphins. StarKist, the largest supplier of canned tuna in the United States, announced: "No dolphins will be harmed or killed in catching StarKist tuna." Other tuna companies promised to change their ways as well.

Congress passed a new law to help consumers know which tuna is caught without harm to dolphins. Tuna cans must have labels to identify "dolphin-safe" tuna. Each canner's logo is different. Look for the words "dolphin-safe."

LONG JOURNEY FOR A SHORT VISIT

After a two-million-year journey, Comet Austin arrived. The new comet was first discovered in December 1989. It promised a bright show in the night skies of April and May. But before long, experts were saying, "Forget it." For technical reasons, the sparkler got dull. When viewed with binoculars during the last two weeks of April, Austin was a dim, fuzzy patch. Once it completes its trip around our Sun, the comet will sail back to where it came from—the distant reaches of the solar system. If it returns at all, it will take millions of years.

HAPPY BIRTHDAY, PLANET EARTH!

On Sunday, April 22, millions of Americans gathered in parks and public places. They marched, sang, joined cleanup crews and listened to speeches about our planet. They were celebrating the 20th anniversary of Earth Day. They were starting a new era of public concern for the environment.

Earth Day in Washington, D.C.

Since the first Earth Day in 1970, the environmental movement has had its ups and downs. Many new laws have been passed to help clean up air and water and protect endangered species. But as the 1980s drew to a close, there were reports about holes in the ozone layer and beaches being polluted. Animals were becoming extinct at an alarming rate. There were disastrous oil spills. Nuclear and toxic wastes were piling up with no place to put them. Tropical rain forests were being burned and bulldozed off the face of the Earth. We were even running out of room for our trash.

Across the country and around the world, people took action. They planted trees. They started recycling programs to save energy and resources. They rode bikes and walked instead of driving. They asked for new laws to clean up our air and water. People everywhere showed they want a cleaner, safer, healthier environment. They hope every day can be Earth Day from now on!

HUBBLE TROUBLE

The largest space telescope ever built was put into orbit on April 24. The Hubble Space Telescope was launched by the U.S. space shuttle *Discovery.* For the next 15 years or so, Hubble was to show us a new view of the universe. It would orbit above the clouds of Earth's atmosphere. That meant getting a much clearer picture of space than ever before.

The Hubble Space Telescope

But soon after the launch, Hubble troubles showed up. A flawed mirror blurred the space telescope's images. Still, Hubble sent detailed images of such distant objects as the core of a galaxy and an area where new stars are forming. Plans were laid for a space shuttle crew to go make repairs on the telescope in 1993.

1990
MAY

HAWAII GLOWS AND GROWS

A flaming river of lava buried a road near the town of Kalapana on the island of Hawaii on May 5. The lava flowed from Hawaii's Kilauea Volcano, the world's most active volcano. The lava flows down the mountain and into the sea. As it hardens, the lava adds new land to the still-growing island of Hawaii.

Lava from Mt. Kilauea slides into town.

SAD NEWS IN MUPPET LAND

The entertainment world lost a bright talent on May 16. Jim Henson, the creator of the Muppets, died of pneumonia. Most people knew very little about him, but millions knew and loved his Muppets.

The Muppets hit *Sesame Street* in 1969. Big Bird, Cookie Monster and Oscar the Grouch seemed so human and witty that parents loved them just as much as kids did. *The Muppet Show*, with Kermit the

Jim Henson

Frog and Miss Piggy, made Henson a superstar in 1976. Three Muppet movies followed. One of Henson's businesses even made costumes and special effects for the 1990 hit film *Teenage Mutant Ninja Turtles*. His bright star may be gone, but Jim Henson's work lives on.

WHO ARE THE HEROES?

World Almanac polled high school kids to see whom they admired in public life. For the first time in the poll's 11-year history, a woman was named as the most admired person. Paula Abdul, the pop music singer and dancer, was named top heroine of young America. Who was in second place? "Mom" won on a write-in vote. Third was Michael Jordan, the basketball star of the Chicago Bulls. Jordan was last year's top winner. Fourth was the write-in vote for "Dad." First Lady Barbara Bush and talk-show host Oprah Winfrey tied for fifth place. Nelson Mandela came in sixth, marking the first time a foreign political leader finished in the top ten. Next were real-estate magnate Donald Trump, President George Bush, actor Tom Cruise and singer Janet Jackson.

RAVES AND FAVES

What was "in" for the kids of 1990? Toons were tops, as kids made *The Simpsons* their number one favorite TV show. They also liked *Teenage Mutant Ninja Turtles* in a big way. Other top TV shows were *The Wonder Years*, *America's Funniest Home Videos*, *The Cosby Show*, *Growing Pains*, *Doogie Howser, M.D.* and *Roseanne*.

Fads included friendship bracelets made of yarn. Favorite fashions included oversize clothes and Simpsons T-shirts. High-top shoes were "in," and so were shoes painted with puff paint or spatter paint. Miniskirts and too-big jeans sagging low on the hips were back from the 1960s.

Kids were listening to rock and rap. New Kids on the Block and Bon Jovi were favorite groups. Other faves were Paula Abdul, Bobby Brown, Janet Jackson and Madonna. M.C. Hammer sold more records than anyone else in 1990.

Kids were worried about the environment, crime, grades, drugs and peer pressure. They were saying "Cool," "Rad," "Cowabunga," "Hang tough," "Peace," "Awesome," "Get real, "Grow a brain" and "Yo." They were crazy about hand-held video games, and Teenage Mutant Ninja Turtles action figures were the best-selling toy line of the year.

OWL ALERT

Spotted owls are in big trouble, and so are the forests that are their home. In June the U.S. Fish and Wildlife Service named the northern spotted owl an endangered species. This means it will be illegal to harm any of the owls or to destroy their habitat. Northern spotted owls are rare. Only 2,000 to 3,000 known pairs remain. Most of them live on federal land in old forests of the Pacific Northwest—Washington, Oregon and northern California. Experts fear that the owl's dwindling numbers are due to logging in old-growth forests, which destroys the owl's habitat.

The ruling raised an uproar. Loggers were angry. They lose their jobs if they are stopped from cutting down trees. Other groups were fighting to save the owl and the old forests. Lawmakers are working to settle this problem so that both the jobs and the owls can be protected.

BUDGET TROUBLES

In June President Bush broke his "Read my lips" pledge not to raise taxes. The nation was drowning in debt. The budget crunch had leaders worried. Despite his vow, the president said tax increases would be needed to help the budget.

George Bush pays lip service.

Jose Canseco, Jr.

BIG BASEBALL BUCKS

Jose Canseco, Jr. became baseball's highest-paid player on June 27. He signed a five-year contract with the Oakland Athletics. He will be paid an average of $4.7 million a year.

FAREWELL TO AMERICA'S OLDEST BALLPARK

On June 29 the Chicago White Sox played their last game at old Comiskey Park. The great park had 80 years of great moments. It was America's oldest major league ballpark. It had the first fireworks-and-light exploding scoreboard. Next season the White Sox would be playing at a brand new Comiskey Park being built across the street. As the game against the Oakland Athletics ended, thousands of fans rose to their feet and sang the White Sox anthem: "Na-na-na-na . . . Na-na-na-na . . . Hey, hey, hey, good-bye."

THE YEAR OF THE NO-HITTER

Nine no-hit baseball games were thrown in 1990. That was two more than the previous record, set in 1908. Nolan Ryan of the Texas Rangers pitched his sixth no-hitter in June. No other pitcher in history had ever thrown more than four no-hitters. And for the first time in history, two no-hit games were pitched on the same day! On June 29 Dave Stewart of the Oakland A's pitched a no-hitter against Toronto in a 5–0 win. Then Los Angeles Dodger Fernando Valenzuela did the same to St. Louis in a 6–0 win.

PROTECT THE OZONE

Leaders from 59 nations meeting in London agreed on June 29 to join in protecting the ozone layer. High above the Earth, the ozone layer protects us from the sun's harmful ultraviolet rays. The ozone layer is being damaged by industrial gases, found in things like air conditioners, foam packaging, refrigerators, insulation and fire extinguishers. By the year 2000 most nations will stop producing the gases that harm the ozone layer.

1990
JULY

Mel Blanc and Bugs Bunny

THAT'S ALL, FOLKS

A tombstone was placed on the Hollywood grave of Mel Blanc in July. Blanc, who performed the voices of Bugs Bunny, Daffy Duck and other beloved cartoon characters, died in 1989 at the age of 81. The new tombstone reads: "That's All, Folks." The quote, made famous by another of Mel's characters, Porky Pig, ended every Warner Brothers cartoon and is a fitting tribute to the man who brought so many memories to people everywhere.

WORLD CUP

A U.S. team played in the 1990 World Cup finals for the first time in 40 years. The World Cup is a battle for the championship of soccer—the most popular sport in the world. Played every four years, it is the biggest sports event in the world. More than one billion of the world's five billion people watched 1990's final World Cup game on television.

National teams from 24 countries play in a month-long tournament. They have to qualify by playing in competition that started two years earlier. The 1990 World Cup was played in 12 different cities in Italy. West Germany won the World Cup in the final game on July 8 in Rome.

Soccer is the fastest-growing sport in the United States. Fans are already looking forward to the next World Cup. It will be held in 1994—in the United States!

TOP GYMNAST

Fourteen-year-old Kim Zmeskal was the top American female gymnast in 1990. Kim won the all-around title at the U.S. Gymnastics Championships in July. She also took the all-around titles at McDonald's American Cup and the U.S. Challenge. In August Kim scored a perfect 10 on the vault at a major meet between the United States and the Soviet Union.

Kim Zmeskal

1990
AUGUST

CRISIS IN THE MIDDLE EAST

On August 2 the small, oil-rich nation of Kuwait was attacked and taken over by Iraq, its larger Persian Gulf neighbor. Iraq's leader was a dictator named Saddam Hussein. His invasion set off a worldwide protest.

Some say that money was the reason for the attack. Iran and Iraq had been at war for eight years. Iraq has large oil reserves, but Saddam Hussein could not sell the oil for enough money to pay his war debts. Food in Iraq was in short supply. Hussein was worried about being overthrown. By seizing Kuwait and its oil fields, the Iraqi dictator had more oil to sell. Hussein claimed that Kuwait belonged to Iraq anyway. Iraq has never recognized Kuwait as a separate country.

Neighboring Saudi Arabia had even more oil than Kuwait. Some Persian Gulf nations worried that Saddam Hussein would take over Saudi Arabia too. Saudi Arabia's king asked President George Bush to send soldiers to defend Saudi Arabia against Iraq.

The U.S. and the United Nations called on Hussein to leave Kuwait. They offered peace plans. They formed a U.N. coalition to prepare a massive ground attack by troops and tanks. Still Hussein refused to leave. The United States and other countries rushed troops, ships and planes to the Persian Gulf area to help free Kuwait. The military operation was named Desert Storm. For months these allied troops prepared for the coming fight with Iraq.

American troops enter Kuwait.

MAGELLAN MAPS VENUS

The spacecraft *Magellan*, launched in 1989, began orbiting Venus in August. Its radar equipment pierces the planet's thick clouds. *Magellan* sends signals back to Earth so scientists can make pictures and maps of Venus. The photos show huge craters on Venus. Some of the craters are the size of Los Angeles and two miles deep! The photos also show piles of windblown dust and a 200-mile-long river made of hardened lava. Venus has many volcanoes, and some of them are active.

The temperature on Venus is about 900° Fahrenheit because of its atmosphere. The atmosphere is made up of carbon dioxide, a heat-trapping gas. Interest in Venus has grown in recent years because of the buildup of carbon dioxide in Earth's atmosphere. Some scientists say this buildup may cause global warming. They may learn more about the process of global warming by studying Venus.

1990
SEPTEMBER

JUICE BOXES ARE OUT

Maine was the first state to ban the sale of juice boxes because of their packaging. Juice boxes are made of layers of bonded paper, plastic and aluminum. The layers are difficult to recycle. Not everyone agreed with the law. Some packaging officials set up test programs to prove that juice boxes can be recycled. Meanwhile, people in a Rhode Island community send the boxes to a recycling plant in New York. The boxes are recycled into plastic lumber.

A NEW MUSEUM

The Ellis Island Museum of Immigration opened on September 9. It honors all immigrants to the United States. It is part of the Statue of Liberty National Monument in New York Harbor. From 1892 until it closed in 1954, Ellis Island was the entry point for more than 12 million people coming to this country. The center screened out newcomers who might not be good citizens. All were checked for health. They were asked for papers to prove they had arrived legally. Those who passed could stay and eventually become citizens. Now the center has been restored and reopened as a museum. Photos, films, exhibits and tapes tell the story of immigration from the first newcomers to the present day.

The United States has received more immigrants than any other country in the world. Nearly half of all Americans living in 1990 are descendants of immigrants who came to the United States through Ellis Island!

Georgians celebrate after Atlanta is chosen as the site of the 1996 Olympics.

ATLANTA AWARDED OLYMPICS

The city of Atlanta, Georgia, learned in September that it had been chosen as the site of the 1996 Summer Olympic Games. Atlanta will become the third U.S. city to host the Summer Olympics. The others were St. Louis (1904) and Los Angeles (1932 and 1984). The XXVI Olympic Games in 1996 will celebrate 100 years of modern Olympic Games!

NEW NC-17 MOVIE RATING

Hollywood created a new category called NC-17 for films containing a lot of violence or other material that may be inappropriate for young viewers. No one under 17 will be admitted to NC-17 films.

WORLD LEADERS HELP CHILDREN

Held in September, the World Summit for Children was the first global meeting devoted to making life better for children. More than 70 countries sent leaders to the summit at the United Nations. They pledged to join in efforts to save the lives of millions of children who die before age five. Goals they hope to reach before the year 2000 include providing safe drinking water and enough food to all families.

They want more governments to sign a treaty called the Convention on the Rights of the Child. The treaty is meant to help protect children from harm and to make sure they receive what they need to grow and mature. Of the 159 countries represented in the U.N., 96 countries have signed the treaty into law. These are some of the rights the treaty lists: The right to have proper food and medical care. The right to be protected against neglect and cruelty. The right to receive a free education. The right to have a name and a nationality. The right to be among the first to receive aid in times of disaster. The right to develop work skills and other abilities. The right to play.

A delegate to the World Summit for Children

1990
OCTOBER

United Germany

GERMANY IS UNITED

East and West Germany merged on October 3 to form a single nation. Germany was divided into Communist and non-Communist states after World War II. The 45-year split ended in a midnight celebration of pealing bells and the singing of national hymns. No longer are the people divided by the Berlin Wall, which split their land between East and West. The black, red and gold flag of the Federal Republic of Germany was raised in front of the new capital city, Berlin. Now Germany is a federal republic in which the people elect their leaders by secret ballot.

TOURISTS FIND DOORS LOCKED

The U.S. budget was in a mess. On October 6 and 7 many government services were closed to cut costs. Tourists on vacation found national parks and monuments closed. From Yosemite National Park to the Florida Everglades, people were turned away. The Smithsonian museums were closed. The Statue of Liberty was empty.

Did the shutdown save money? Some experts felt the closings may have cost more than they saved. Millions of dollars in camping fees, road tolls and sales at museum shops were lost. And many people were upset by ruined vacation plans.

DISCOVERY LAUNCHES *ULYSSES*

The U.S. space shuttle *Discovery* took off on October 6. The smooth lift-off was good news for NASA. Shuttle launchings had been grounded since early summer due to fuel leaks. One mission of *Discovery*'s astronauts was to send the space probe *Ulysses* to the Sun. If you could travel as fast as *Ulysses*, you'd go across the United States from New York to Los Angeles

Discovery *returns from a successful mission.*

in 4 $^1/_2$ minutes. *Ulysses* will race out to Jupiter and use that planet's gravity to fling itself into a new vertical orbit. In 1994 *Ulysses* will fly over the Sun's south pole. In 1995 it will pass over the north pole. It will measure the Sun's magnetic field. It will measure X-rays and radio waves emitted by the Sun and conduct other experiments.

TROUBLES IN THE SOVIET UNION

All year, the Soviet Union struggled with disorder. President Mikhail Gorbachev tried to keep his reform policies alive. The Soviet Union's 15 republics made growing demands for greater self-government. And the economy was crumbling. Many people were jobless. Prices soared. Shortages of food, medicine, fuel and supplies worsened.

Russians demand change.

Why was the Soviet Union in such trouble? For many years, the government owned everything in the country. It owned the farms, factories, businesses and property. It set prices and salaries. People produced only what they were told to produce. Gorbachev began to change this system when he took over in 1985. The Soviet Union began to move toward a free-market economy. It began shifting state-owned businesses to private control. But change didn't happen fast enough. It led to what one expert called an "awesome, awesome mess." The switch to the market economy would have its best chance of success if political reform came with it. Gorbachev offered the republics greater power, hoping to gain their cooperation. But disorder spread, and the republics grew more rebellious.

NOT SUCH A HONEY OF A BEE

A swarm of dangerous bees entered the United States in October from Mexico. Called Africanized bees, these bees are very much like the more common European bee found throughout the United States. However, the Africanized bees may not produce as much honey as the European bees, and they also may not pollinate crops as well. If the Africanized bees were to mix with the European bees, it might mean less honey and fewer crops.

The dangerous bees look nearly the same as European honey bees. Their sting is no more poisonous, but the Africanized bees are more likely to attack, sometimes in large groups of up to 150 bees. For this reason they are sometimes called killer bees, although very few people have actually been killed by them.

GORBACHEV WINS NOBEL PEACE PRIZE

Mikhail Gorbachev of the Soviet Union won the Nobel Peace Prize for 1990. The Soviet leader was chosen for his efforts to ease global tensions. He championed political change in Eastern Europe and helped to end the cold war.

UNDERDOGS SWEEP WORLD SERIES

Baseball experts didn't give the Cincinnati Reds much respect during the 1990 baseball season. But the Reds did what everyone said they could never do. They won their first division title since 1979. Then they beat the awesome Oakland Athletics in the World Series. The Reds won the first four games for a World Series sweep. The Athletics became the first team to get swept in a World Series the year after sweeping one.

The Cincinnati Reds take the title.

1990
NOVEMBER

WRANGLE OVER KING HOLIDAY

In November Arizona voters turned down plans to create a Martin Luther King holiday. Most states celebrate the birthday of Dr. Martin Luther King, Jr. on the third Monday in January. Arizona, Montana and New Hampshire do not observe the King holiday.

Marchers in support of Martin Luther King, Jr.

When Arizona said no to a King birthday holiday, the state lost millions of dollars in tourist business. Directors of events such as the NBA All-Star basketball game and the 1993 Super Bowl decided to avoid Arizona because of the King decision. Many of the players are African-Americans. They didn't want to play in a state that refused to honor the slain civil rights leader. Some lawmakers vowed to add the holiday without the voters' approval. People who didn't want the holiday said they would fight such a move.

EARTH DESERVES A BREAK TODAY

McDonald's announced in November that it would switch to paper packaging. McDonald's was one of the world's biggest users of polystyrene, the material used to make foam packaging. The "billions served" meant a heap of Big Mac polystyrene containers. Many end up in landfills. Tons more end up in the ocean, where sea mammals eat it instead of food, and starve. And the gases used to make some polystyrene foam can break down the Earth's ozone layer.

Action-minded kids played a big part in the decision. They protested and McDonald's listened. Why did McDonald's decide to stop making boxes out of polystyrene? "Our customers just don't feel good about it," admitted the president of the company.

NEW LAW LIMITS TV ADS

The Children's Television Act became a law in November. It limits the number of commercials that can be shown in an hour. On weekend shows the law allows 10 1/2 minutes of ads in an hour. On weekday shows it allows 12 minutes of ads in an hour. Before the law was passed, there were no limits.

By the time most children are 18 years old, they will have seen more than 200,000 TV commercials. Experts say that many children can't tell the difference between the ads and the programs. The new law means that children will be watching fewer ads and more educational shows.

AMERICA'S AIR TO BE CLEANER

The Clean Air Act of 1990 was signed into law in November. It focuses on three main areas of air pollution: acid rain, smog and toxic chemicals. The law updates and tightens federal air-pollution standards for the first time since 1977. It will mean cleaner emissions from cars, power plants, factories and fuels that are burned.

When President George Bush signed the Clean Air Act, he said, "Every American expects and deserves to breathe clean air." By the year 2000, according to the law, Americans will be breathing cleaner air.

TROOPS ON GUARD IN THE DESERT

On November 29 the U.N. Security Council set a January 15 deadline for Iraq to leave Kuwait. More than 500,000 troops, 100 ships and about 900 planes were in the Persian Gulf. The troops were there to protect Saudi Arabia from invasion by Iraq and to force Iraq to get out of Kuwait.

A few of the 500,000 troops on duty in the Gulf

1990
DECEMBER

The Chunnel

WORLD'S LONGEST UNDERWATER TUNNEL

In 1987 giant tunnel-boring machines began digging an underwater tunnel to connect England and France. Finally, on December 1, British and French workers met beneath the English Channel. After knocking out a hole big enough to walk through, they exchanged flags to celebrate.

The English Channel Tunnel, or Chunnel, runs underwater for 23 ½ miles (37.8 kilometers). It is the longest underwater tunnel in the world. The Chunnel will actually be three tunnels when completed. Two of the tunnels will be for trains carrying cargo and people between France and England. The third tunnel, completed in October 1990, will service and repair the other two. Trains are expected to run through the Chunnel starting in June 1993. When the Chunnel is done, people should be able to board a train in London, England, and reach Paris, France, in three hours. That's about half the time it now takes by train and boat between the two cities.

SEA LIONS PAY A VISIT

Hundreds of sea lions migrated to San Francisco in December. The sea lions climbed onto docks in San Francisco Bay. Plenty of herring, a favorite food, swam nearby, so the sea lions were happy. Tourists were happy because the sea lions were fun to watch. Nearby businesses were happy because the tourists who came to see the sea lions spent money in their stores. But some people in San Francisco couldn't stand the sea lions! They said the animals were noisy, dirty and smelly. Getting rid of them would not be easy. A law protects sea lions from harm by people. They hope the sea lions don't come back next December!

Macaulay Culkin

THE MILLION-DOLLAR KID

Ten-year-old Macaulay Culkin was the hit of the Christmas season with his movie *Home Alone*. The John Hughes comedy is about a young boy who outwits a pair of bungling burglars after accidentally being left at home when his family goes on vacation. It set new box office records and became one of the highest-grossing films of all time. Young Mac is now commanding over a million dollars for his films!

Eduard Shevardnadze gives his resignation speech.

A SOVIET BOMBSHELL

On December 20 Soviet Foreign Minister Eduard Shevardnadze resigned. Beset by a crumbling economy and increasing demands for independence from the 15 Soviet republics, Mikhail Gorbachev had tightened his grip on the country. Shevardnadze quit in protest, saying, "The reformers have headed for the hills. Dictatorship is coming. No one knows what kind of dictatorship it will be, who will come to power." As the year came to a close, people everywhere held their breath waiting to see what the future of the powerful Soviet Union would be.

INDEX